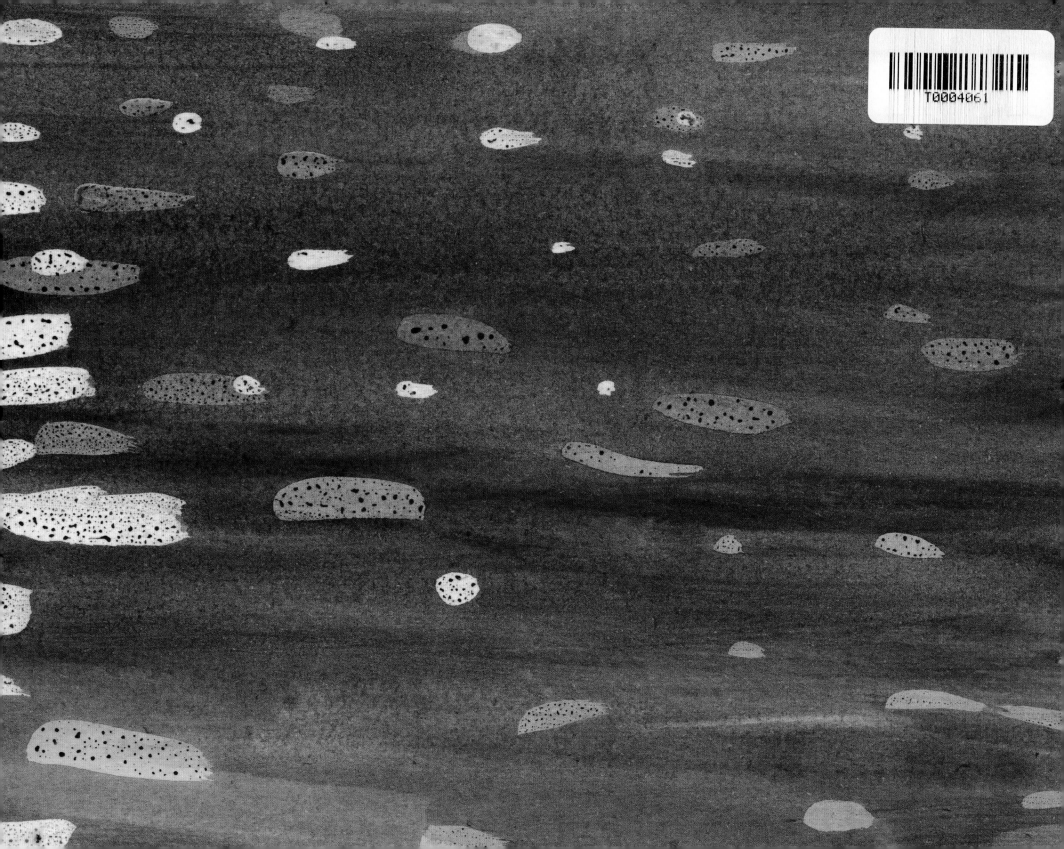

To my parents, for their support and love of nature

First published in 2023 by Child's Play (International) Ltd
Ashworth Road, Bridgemead, Swindon SN5 7YD, UK

Published in USA in 2023 by Child's Play Inc
250 Minot Avenue, Auburn, Maine 04210
US English adaptation by MaryChris Bradley

Distributed in Australia by Child's Play Australia Pty Ltd
Unit 10/20 Narabang Way, Belrose, Sydney, NSW 2085

ISBN 978-1-78628-472-3
L240323CPL06234723

Printed and bound in Heshan, China

1 3 5 7 9 10 8 6 4 2

A catalogue record of this book is available from the British Library

www.childs-play.com

life on the
Thames

Emma Shoard

From Source to Sea

Ashton Keynes

Source of the Thames

Cricklade

Chimney Meadows

Oxford

Abingdon

Marlow

Windsor

Henley-on-Thames

Goring

Hartslock

Reading

This is the River Thames, one of the most famous rivers in the world. Join me as we follow its ancient path across England, west to east, from its source to the sea.

Many people think of it as a river at the center of a big city, dark and dirty, but the full story of the Thames reveals so much more.

The Thames was frozen during the ice ages and flowed into Europe long before ancient Britain became an island.

In those times long past, it's believed that a host of creatures, including hippos, mammoths, and rhinos, lived along its banks, parts of which were tropical swamps or thick forests.

Dengie Peninsula

Southend-on-Sea

London

Tower Bridge

Billingsgate Market

Canvey Island

Isleworth

London Bridge

Thames Barrier

Teddington Lock

Richmond Park

Gravesend

Hoo Peninsula

Rochester

Isle of Sheppey

On our journey along the Thames of today, we will encounter fish, insects, birds, and mammals, some you already know, others will be new to you, and a few might have underwater lives you never imagined.

The Source of the Thames

Where does the River Thames begin? A stone marks the official spot in a field near the Gloucestershire village of Kemble, but in recent, much drier times, the source is often as much as five miles downstream. When water does bubble out of the ground, it muddies the field, puddles, then begins its journey toward the sea. It is strange to think this little stream that appears and disappears among the grasses, nettles, and young willow trees will become a great river, but life crowds around it from the beginning.

This is also the start of the Thames Path, a long-distance, national walking trail that follows the river to London, where it links to a new path to the sea. Filled with countless natural beauty spots, wildlife, and history, there are helpful signposts along the way.

Thames Path
185.2 miles long

This part of the river is best explored on foot, and if you crouch down you can enjoy a duck's-eye view of all the fascinating creatures and plant life.

Pink-speckled snake's-head fritillaries (from the lily family) once carpeted the Thames' wet meadows in the spring, but most of the country's wild population now grows in Cricklade's North Meadow, a National Nature Reserve.

Ducks

Ducks love water! They are one of the first animals you will see taking advantage of this watery habitat the length of the Thames. Their quacking conversations are the soft, bubbly soundtrack of the river.

Mallards are the most common duck species by far and they are beautiful birds. They appear happy to live alongside us humans, and because of this, we occasionally get the chance to see them grow from tiny ducklings into adult birds.

In the spring, mallards will build their nests in sheltered spots near the river. After the female lays her eggs, she will sit and incubate them for 28 days, only getting up to eat or stretch her legs. When the ducklings hatch, they remain in the nest for just one day before their mother leads them to the water.

They eat plants, including seeds and berries, insects, and other small creatures, feeding on the surface or ducking underwater to reach something tasty, leaving their bottoms sticking up.

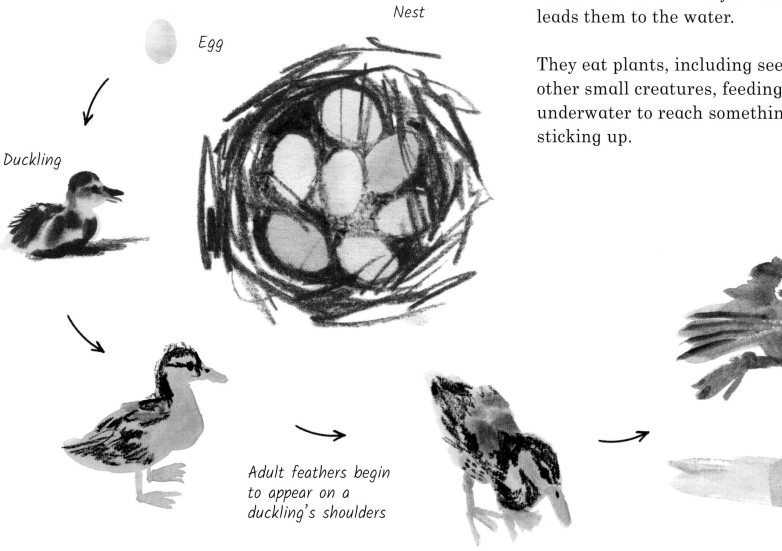

Egg

Nest

Duckling

Adult feathers begin to appear on a duckling's shoulders

Mallards use their wide bill to find food in the water

Male ducks are known as *drakes*. With their bolder markings and a bright, iridescent green head that can give off a purple sheen, they stand out from the mottled brown females.

They have a bright blue stripe on their wings

Webbed feet help them paddle

Ducklings

Ducks and other waterfowl have *precocial* chicks. This means they're ready to walk, swim, and feed themselves when they are born, though they do need their mother to guide them at first. They are covered in soft feathers, called *down*, which protects them if they tumble out of the nest and onto the ground.

Although the ducklings can swim right away, their feathers aren't yet waterproof, so they spend lots of time out of the water, drying off and getting warm next to or under their mother. The parents are protective and will fight off other animals competing with their family for food or space.

Moorhens and Coots

Alongside the ducks, you may see coots and moorhens. These two species are closely related, but there are easy ways to tell them apart. The more common coots are completely black except for their white beak and shield. Moorhens are smaller and have a red shield and a yellow-tipped beak.

Coots are social and bold, often chasing each other with a loud call, a bit like a bark! Their feet are large and not webbed, but shaped to help them walk on marshy ground. Moorhens are quieter but show off their white undertail feathers by flicking them as they walk. The chicks of both have fluffy, round bodies and large feet.

Coots   Moorhens

Otters

As well as being home to some of our most common animals, the Thames is also where some of our rarest animals live. If you are lucky, you might see a wild otter! These elusive, secretive, and playful creatures can appear on the water's surface, then silently slip away, their smooth bodies barely making a ripple. Perhaps they hide from us because they were hunted by humans in the past.

Otters belong to the same family of mammals as weasels and badgers, but unlike those woodland animals, they are more at home in the river. Otters with their webbed feet are excellent swimmers, agile, fast, and strong. But they aren't born with this skill. Mother and cubs stay together for more than a year while she teaches her young to swim and hunt.

Living near water, an otters' favorite food is fish, but they aren't fussy, and will also eat crustaceans, amphibians, waterbirds, and insects.

Long whiskers help detect prey

Streamlined head and body

Very strong jaws can bite through shell and bone

Otter fur is so thick that only the outer layer gets wet when they swim. Air bubbles trapped in their fur creates a layer that keeps their woolly undercoat dry and warm. Otters curl up in an underground burrow, called a *holt*, when they need to dry off and sleep.

Watch for otter-size paths through riverbank plants, as they like to make their home among vegetation like tangled tree roots and rocky openings. Another sign is their *spraint* (poo), which they leave in open spaces or tall grasses to mark their territory and send scented messages to each other.

Snakes

Adult barred
grass snake

Green with distinctive
yellow and black
collar of scales

Tongue flicks out to
taste scents in the air

Along the riverbank is another hunter. Barred grass
snakes are one of only three snake species in the UK
and can grow to more than three feet long! Although
they are predators, you don't have to be afraid of
them as they have no fangs or venom.

Their favorite prey are frogs, toads, and newts,
which they catch in the water and swallow
whole. They also like small fish and birds.
Snakes are excellent swimmers and can often
be spotted sidewinding, holding their heads just
above the water's surface like a periscope.

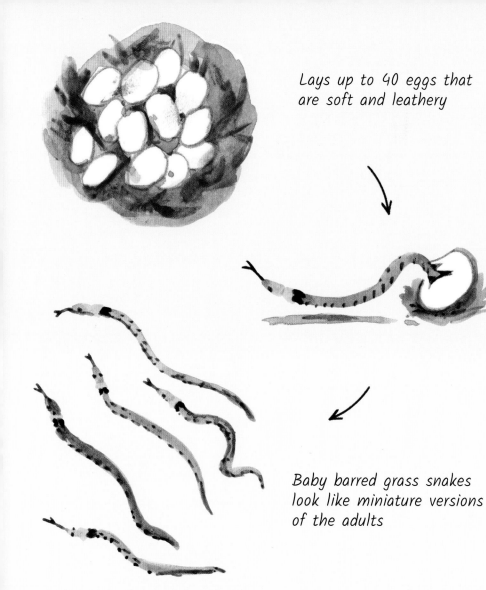

Lays up to 40 eggs that are soft and leathery

Baby barred grass snakes look like miniature versions of the adults

Snakes are cold-blooded and often bask in the sun's heat. The sun also provides them with necessary vitamins and minerals. In winter or cold weather, they curl up underground, going into a state similar to hibernation. They emerge in the spring to find a mate. In summer, they build a nest somewhere warm near water—usually in rotting wood and leaves—where the females lay their eggs.

Smaller than barred grass snakes, European common adders are about two feet long, with dark zigzag markings and red eyes. They are the only venomous species of snake in the UK, but despite their frightening appearance, they rarely bite humans, preferring to avoid us altogether, saving their venom for their prey. Sensing the vibrations of our footsteps, they slip away before being seen.

Unlike the *oviparous* barred grass snake that lays eggs, European common adders are *viviparous* and give birth to live young. This is a special adaptation in snakes living in colder climates that allows their developing young to be kept warm inside the mother's body.

European common adder

Water voles

Water voles are another secretive resident of the riverbank, sheltering from predators among the reeds and burrowing into the soft mud to make their homes. This species of rodent likes dense vegetation, but riverside developments have changed the banks, creating hard, artificial barriers along the water. Rising numbers of predators—including the American mink, introduced to the countryside by humans—have also threatened the water voles' survival. Their numbers are now disturbingly low, but conservation work is being done to help create safer spaces for them in the wild.

Populations can be seen in a few places along the Upper Thames. If you find a quiet spot, you might just see movement on the opposite bank as a water vole plops into the water and swims through the weeds on the surface. Their fur is thick and buoyant, fluffed with air to stay waterproof and warm.

Small eyes, long sensitive whiskers

Water voles can be mistaken for rats, but they are quite different. They are smaller, with rounder faces, and their furry paws, tail, and hidden ears are brown, while rats' paws, tail, and ears are pink.

Rat

Water vole

Wagtails

There are several species of wagtails, including three in the UK: yellow, pied, and my favorite, gray. Gray wagtails are fascinating little birds that can be easily found near fast-flowing water.

Nest near water in sheltered cracks in rocks or buildings

Pointed beak for catching insects in flight

Both parents gather insects to feed the chicks

Elegant and distinctive in their movements, their long tail feathers bob as though they are balancing—even when they are standing still.

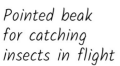

Yellow wagtail   Pied wagtail

Gray wagtails have the longest tail of the three and their feathers are a mixture of soft gray, yellow, and white.

They flit fairy-like by the river, snatching insects like midges and flies out of the air. They fly low, as they swoop up and down. Spotting these traits is the best way to identify them.

Kingfishers

Spectacular kingfishers, with their bright blue and shiny copper-colored feathers, can be quite difficult to spot, preferring the peace and quiet away from human activity. The best way to find them is to learn about their habitat. Fortunately, there are plenty of places along the Thames— like low branches hanging over calm water—where they like to perch while fishing.

Kingfishers sit motionless, pointing their sharp beak downward, looking for underwater prey. They will tuck in their wings like a dart, eyes fixed on the fish until the last possible moment, and just before hitting the water, they protect their eyes by closing a third, transparent eyelid. Then they quickly surface with the fish. It's all over in a flash of blue!

Kingfisher chicks, unlike *precocial* ducklings, are *altricial*—helpless at first and reliant on their parents. The chicks stay sheltered in a burrow deep in the riverbank, while both parents bring small fish, feeding them in rotation. When they leave the nest, the fledglings will be fed for about four days. After that, the parents chase the young away before starting another brood.

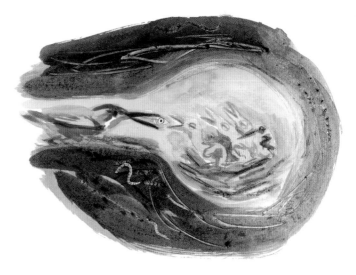

Nest in burrows dug 2-3 feet into a riverbank

Chicks stay in the nest for about a month

Minnows and
sticklebacks

Perch

Crayfish

Roach

Pike

Underwater

Beneath the river's surface, the cold, clear water is full of tiny plants and animals, as well as carefully camouflaged fish and invertebrates. Many blend in with the mud and gravel or hide under rocks and in the weeds. The light bouncing off the ripples at the top keeps their movements hidden.

At the bottom is the layered riverbed. Organic matter drifts down from plants and animals, mixing with the mud and silt. Beneath that soft layer are small stones polished by the water's movement, followed by larger stones, then the clay and rock, including chalk that was laid down before the river even existed.

Insects

The stunning chalk-hill meadows that slope down to the Thames are part of a special natural habitat—the Goring Gap—where wildflowers grow, including rare orchids.

Brimstone

Adonis blue

Brown hairstreak

Grizzled skipper

Green hairstreak

Orange tip

Pictured are a few of the beautiful butterflies and moths you might see there. Beginning life as *larvae* (caterpillars), they grow fat, eating lots of leaves before encasing themselves in a cocoon or *chrysalis* from which they will emerge as a colorful winged insect. This incredible transformation is called *metamorphosis*.

Just above the water, the air is filled with the papery bodies of insects, from tiny midges to dragonflies. In spring and summer, we can hear dragonflies' large, lacy wings click-clacking as they race past us, hunting in the air. Dragonflies and the smaller damselflies also transform. Most of their lives are spent underwater as nymphs, before they gradually become winged adults. Nymphs crawl out of the water and shed their old skin, leaving the ghostly outer case on a stem. They unfold their new wings to begin a second life. When they are still, dragonflies keep their wings outstretched, while damselflies fold theirs in line with their abdomen.

Flying insect populations in the UK and around the world are in serious decline. Though it isn't difficult for us to create habitats for these small creatures, they are extremely sensitive to our impact on the environment. Pesticides—designed to stop insects from eating our crops—can easily spread from the farm and into the environment, causing a lot of harm.

Adult dragonfly

Emerging dragonfly

Dragonfly eggs

Nymphs

Bats

The glow of the city is on the horizon now, and the wooded islands—called *aits* or *eyots*—are dark and still. As night falls, bats begin to swoop over the water, caught in the soft moonlight between the shadowy shelter of the trees.

Daubenton's bats often roost in tunnels, tree hollows, stone buildings, and bridges

*Mother bats
and their young
form large groups*

There are 18 bat species in the UK. Pictured here are Daubenton's bats, also known as *water bats*. This is the perfect place for these insect-eating mammals to hunt, and it is thrilling to watch their fast, erratic flight.

Once we know there are bats around, we can identify them with a small device—called *echolocation* or *bio sonar*—that picks up the high-pitched sounds they make. Impossible for humans to hear, these sounds are vital to bats. They use them to communicate, detect prey, and see in the dark. The clicking sounds they make bounce back off objects like an echo, which allows them to build an image of their surroundings so that they can pinpoint and catch insects in the dark.

Locks and Narrowboats

The Thames may seem to meander naturally through the landscape, but the humans living along these banks have made numerous changes for their own benefit. At many points along the river you will come across a lock. A lock is a structure built to control the water level to allow boats to travel safely. The simple design of the *pound lock* has remained the same for hundreds of years.

The long, colorful boats seen on the river through Oxfordshire, Berkshire, and in canals around London are narrowboats, built to fit the tight locks of the UK. During the Industrial Revolution, narrowboats were essential, transporting goods around the country on a huge network of rivers and canals, often with an entire family living in the small back cabin.

Boat enters

Lower gates close

Water fills the chamber

Upper gates open

The lock gates hold back the flow of water and create a chamber, where the level can be controlled by slowly letting water in or out

Life on a narrowboat was hard work, much of it done outdoors, regardless of the weather. The workers had their own community, which was sometimes romanticized, but they knew the river better than anyone. Living on the water, they learned to recognize the rise and fall of the currents and tides, to track the shifting waterline through floods and droughts, and to notice the changes in the seasons.

Narrowboats soon began to be made out of metal rather than wood, and to be powered by steam or diesel, but they could not compete for long with the new railways. Narrowboats could not grow any larger than the locks they had to pass through, and it became faster and cheaper to move goods in other ways. Though many were abandoned or filled in, there are still many working canals around the country today, and people still live onboard converted narrowboats.

Common knots

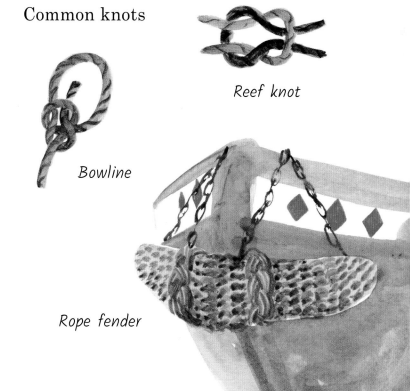

Reef knot

Bowline

Rope fender

Swans

Just before we pass through the largest
lock along the Thames at Teddington,
let's stop to admire the swans.

Known as the Arcadian Thames, this part
of the river feels fitting to be their home.
It is a paradise sitting beside royal palaces
and the old monarchs' hunting grounds.
Here, the white swans glide elegantly
among the weeping willows.

Swans have been symbols of purity in Greek mythology;
they have stood alongside lions, dragons, and unicorns
on coats of arms; and starred as centerpieces of lavish
Tudor banquets. Highly valued, most were the property
of rich families, with the Crown having the right to any
unmarked swans.

So, what is their true nature? Observing these birds
on the shores of the Thames, they walk with their
smaller duck and goose cousins, confident but calm.
They are rarely aggressive, unlike the geese
who like to show the smaller birds who's boss!

Swans mate for life, and you can see
them moving together, mirror images
of each other. In the spring, they
nest and lay eggs, which both
parents will incubate.
After they hatch,
the young swans—
called *cygnets*—
are looked after
by both parents.

Herons

Gray herons are tall and statuesque, and can be found all along the Thames. They stand in the shallows, still and focused, patiently waiting for their prey to come along. They are effective hunters, catching mainly fish, but also feeding on small birds and mammals.

Though usually seen hunting alone, they are sociable, often forming large groups during breeding called *heronries*. They fill lofty trees with large, twiggy nests, high in the branches. Gray herons lay three or four eggs, and you can see their chicks in early spring on Isleworth Ait.

Isleworth Ait

An important nature reserve, it is dense with trees, such as the willow, sycamore, elder, holly, and hawthorn—a haven for wildlife.

As one of the few Thames islands left almost entirely to nature, it is home to many birds and bats, as well as two rare snail species. There is a working boatyard in the backwater, and the osier willows—used for weaving baskets—still stand among the wild trees.

Canada goose

Graylag goose

Egyptian goose

Past Thames

London would not be the same without the Thames. Since ancient times, the river has greeted people from around the globe, with settlers, traders, and invaders all making their way upriver from the sea to what became the capital of the UK.

People have lived in the area for thousands of years, and a bridge—in various forms—has crossed the river here since Roman times. One bridge—completed in 1209—stood here for hundreds of years. It was famous for its arches, as well as its markets, haberdashers, silversmiths, inns, bookshops, chapels, and homes.

The bridge's buildings, held together by wooden beams and pegs, sometimes tumbled into the river, burned down, or were destroyed on purpose. Just as often, rebuilding would start again. Throughout history, the sounds of the rapids rushing through the arches, horses' hooves, and shouting merchants were the norm. From east to west, barges and ships arrived, bringing exotic animals, food, spices, and people from all around the globe.

Some winters were so cold, the vessels froze in place! Delighted Londoners would stream onto the ice to celebrate with a *Frost Fair*, eating, drinking, and playing games.

Mudlarkling

Fragments of London's history have piled up at the water's edge, collecting in layers on the muddy riverbed. Twice a day, the tide goes out to reveal a variety of objects including clay pipes, coins, pottery, oyster shells and animal bones. Someone searching on the shore is called a *mudlark*. Originally, mudlarks were children or poor people seeking items of value—that had fallen from cargo ships or been dropped by ferry passengers—that they could sell or trade.

Today, mudlarking is more about looking for objects that tell the stories of those who lived by the river in the past. There's something magical about anything that sits untouched in the mud until the river decides to reveal it to us. Who drank from this bottle? Whose mantlepiece did this once decorate? Who wore the coat once attached to this button? How long ago did they live?

Clay pipe

Patterned glass

Pottery fragments

Staffordshire combed slipwear

Cowrie shell

Glass bottle

Mussel shell

London Thames

You may think this is the point where wildlife makes way for human civilization, but the Thames is one of the cleanest urban rivers in Europe, and the life we have seen so far continues through the city and out to the sea. But this wasn't always the case.

During the 1950s, much of the Thames was declared *biologically dead*—lacking the oxygen vital to support fish and plant life. Without organisms lower on the food chain, larger animals also had nothing to eat. How did things get so bad?

Throughout history, London used the Thames as a sewer. This wasn't so bad when the population was small, but as the numbers grew and people spread out—building on farmland and marsh, moving from country to city—it became a smelly problem! People were also dumping all kinds of garbage into the river, adding to the pollution.

When the *Great Stink of 1858* almost shut down the Houses of Parliament, it forced the construction of a proper sewer system, but sewage was only part of the problem. In the following 100 years, power stations and factories were built in the city center and the river became polluted again, a bad situation for people's health and for the remaining wildlife.

Today, thanks to more than 50 years of hard work, learning about the river, and protecting it, many fish, waterfowl, and even seals have returned. Over the centuries, the London Thames has been a source of food and water, a highway, a drain, an ice rink, a fairground, and a dump, but thankfully, the environment has finally taken center stage.

Fish

The fish you see here are just a few of the more than 100 species that spend all or part of their lives in the tidal part of the Thames, sometimes known as the Tideway. This part of the river begins at Teddington Lock where the tides bring seawater upstream, supplying the river through London with brackish water, a mixture of fresh and salt water.

This is a critical breeding ground for many species, such as smelts—small shimmery fish that some say smell like cucumber!

Perch

Dace

Smelt

Barbel

European eel

Common goby

Sand goby

Eggs and juvenile smelt

Sprat

Lamprey

Bass

Roach

Some species, like flounders and sea bass, will eventually make their way out to sea to live as adults in the saltwater. Others, like short-snouted seahorses, will spend their entire life here.

Whiting

Seahorse

Flounder

Pipefish

Fishing

Boats that have sailed on the Thames over time include skiffs, clinkers, barges, shallops, peterboats, whiffs, and schooners. Thames barge design was developed over many years, aided by the local knowledge of crews and skippers that has been passed down for generations.

Peterboats, which no longer exist, were small, double-ended fishing boats with a well in the center to keep the fish in the water until they reached market.

Old Billingsgate Market

Peterboat

Thames barge

Market porter and porter's badge

This famous fish market was officially recognized as such by an Act of Parliament in 1699. Located dockside hundreds of years ago, it became a covered market in 1850, and finally moved to Canary Wharf in 1982, where it sells fish from around the globe.

BILLINGSGATE EXOTIC FISH-LTD
OFFICE - 62

MACKEREL (x4)
£20

New Billingsgate Market,
Canary Wharf

Thames Barrier

Built between 1974 and 1982 to protect London from flooding, the Thames Barrier stretches a third of a mile across the river. Of the ten steel gates, the four largest are 200 feet wide and weigh 3,696 tons. It protects 48.3 square miles of central London during tidal and storm surges. Then, when conditions improve, the barrier's gates can be lowered again.

There have been many improvements and developments along the Thames Path in recent years, offering walkers even more to enjoy and explore. Until 2022, the path ended at the Thames Barrier, but it now extends to Woolwich to join the new England Coast Path in a continuous route to the Grain on the Kent coast. Connecting London to the sea, it is the first Source to Sea National Trail in the UK, covering a total distance of 232 miles.

We sail past old warehouses, factories, docks, and Trinity Buoy's Experimental Lighthouse. These are followed by land dug up, filled in, and recolonized by nature. Finally, leaving London, you enter a landscape full of big skies, wet fogs, and drifting mists.

Thames Barrier with gate raised

Lift

Gate

Riverbed

Life Cycle of the Eel

I've always found eels mysterious. In ancient times, some believed these fish came out of the mud fully formed; others thought that horsehair dangled in the water would transform into eels. While we know these stories are myths, the truth about where the Thames' eels come from is almost as incredible.

European eels make a journey of thousands of miles from a place on the other side of the Atlantic called the Sargasso Sea. Here, their eggs hatch into tiny feather-like larvae, which then drift with other young sea life in the ocean currents until they arrive on our shores as baby or glass eels. Next, they swim into estuaries and up rivers, out of the salt water and into fresh water. In their new environment, they become juvenile eels known as *elver*, before they grow into larger yellow eels. They spend most of their life in this young adult form in rivers like the Thames.

When they are fully grown, the silver eels swim out to sea and make the journey all the way back to the place where they were born! There, they mate and spawn before their life ends, and the cycle begins once again.

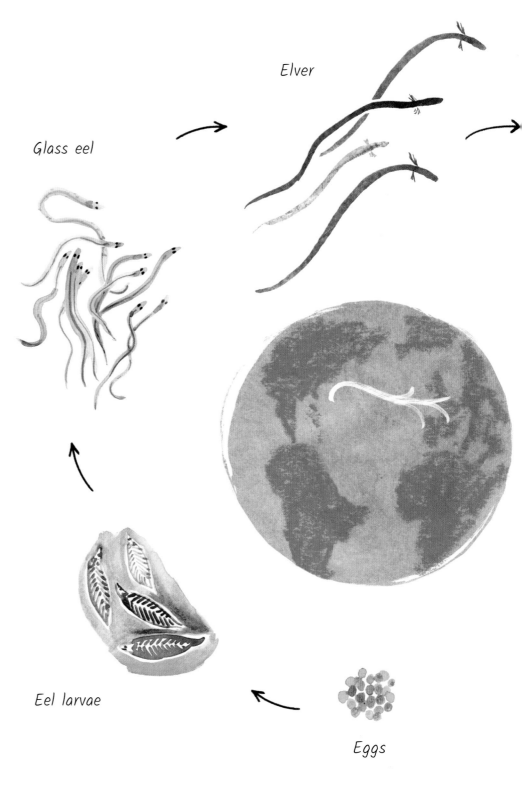

Glass eel

Elver

Eel larvae

Eggs

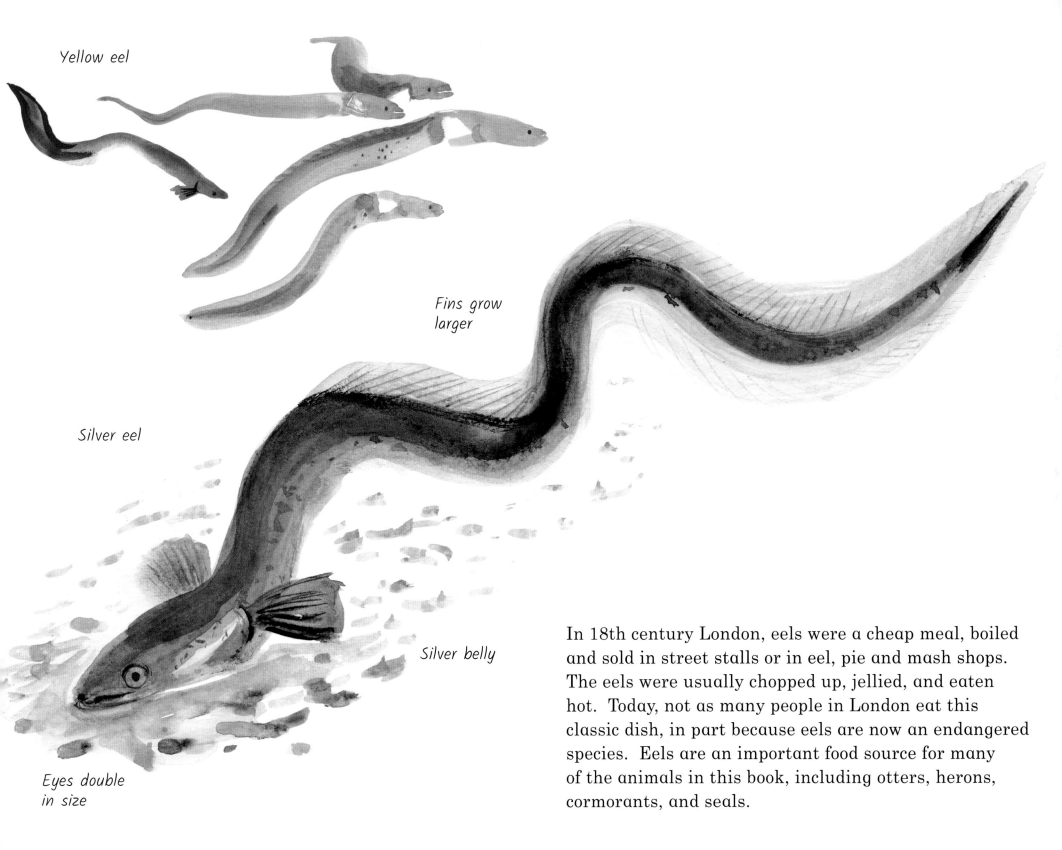

Yellow eel

Fins grow larger

Silver eel

Silver belly

Eyes double in size

In 18th century London, eels were a cheap meal, boiled and sold in street stalls or in eel, pie and mash shops. The eels were usually chopped up, jellied, and eaten hot. Today, not as many people in London eat this classic dish, in part because eels are now an endangered species. Eels are an important food source for many of the animals in this book, including otters, herons, cormorants, and seals.

Thames Estuary

Pull on your boots, wear a hat, and bring your binoculars!
You have reached the section of the Thames where it meets the
sea—the estuary. The river widens, the landscape flattens, and
the human population spreads out.

In the past, it was a hard place to live, with the wind blowing
salt from the sea and the land so soft and boggy. Here, the
tides—caused by the moon's gravitational pull—make the river
flow backward half the day, before turning to rush out to sea
again. This mixes the river's fresh water with the sea's salt
water, creating a different habitat than the ones you have
explored so far.

Grasses and coastal plants living in these unusual conditions
create salt marshes by trapping silt and mud. Numerous
species rely on this rare habitat and the waters here are a
nursery for young fish. Many will stay hidden in the reeds and
shallow pools. If they venture out too far, they might end up
as food for another animal—perhaps a migrating, long-legged
wading bird heading south.

Sea aster

Coltsfoot

Glasswort or samphire

Seals

Can you see the rounded, dark shapes on the shore? As you look harder, watch for a little movement. Could it be a buoy or a log? Then, a flick of a flipper or flare of a nostril tells you that you're staring at seals. And they are staring right back at you, equally curious!

You can spot seals far upriver, even beyond the Houses of Parliament, but the best places to find them are the beaches of the Kent and Essex coasts. Gray seals and breeding harbor (or common) seals have returned to the Thames, and their numbers are increasing thanks to projects that have cleaned up the river, creating a habitat for the large quantity of fish that seals eat.

Baby seals, called pups, are born in summer

Harbor seal pups can swim just a few hours after being born

Pups put on weight quickly by drinking their mother's rich milk

Young seal pups are vulnerable and rely on their mother for food and warmth, but because harbor seal pups can swim as soon as the tide rises, they are better adapted for life on the Thames.

Harbor seal

Gray seal

Their eyes have round lenses (like fish) that allow them to see clearly while underwater

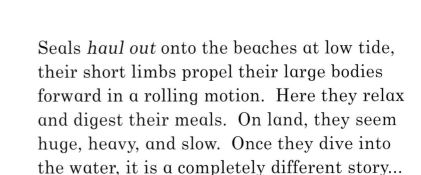

You can tell harbor and gray seals apart by their face shape and size. Harbor seals often lie on their belly or side in a distinctive banana curve and are smaller than gray seals

Seals *haul out* onto the beaches at low tide, their short limbs propel their large bodies forward in a rolling motion. Here they relax and digest their meals. On land, they seem huge, heavy, and slow. Once they dive into the water, it is a completely different story...

Harbor seals have V-shaped nostrils

Their long, sensitive whiskers help them detect and catch prey

Seals and Cetaceans

Underwater, seals are fast, acrobatic creatures and effective hunters. They have excellent vision and hearing in dark waters, which—along with their super-sensitive whiskers—gives them powerful skills, perfect for catching lots of fish. A thick layer of blubber protects them from the cold.

Cetaceans are the family of marine mammals—whales, dolphins and porpoises. Harbor porpoises have also returned to the Thames Estuary. Along with seals and dolphins, they compete for the increasing numbers of fish. The larger seals and dolphins may even attack the porpoises. They are no longer hunted by humans for blubber, but continue to be endangered by old fishing nets, plastic, and noise pollution.

Seal

Dolphin

Porpoise

Though well adapted to life underwater, seals are mammals and must come up to the surface to breathe. Gray seals can hold their breath for up to 16 minutes and harbor seals up to 30. During that time they store oxygen in their blood and muscles, lower their heart rate, and close their nostrils.

We don't know everything about their lives beneath the river's surface, but it is wonderful to know they are there.

Oysters

I have found some amazing oyster shells among the pipes and pottery pieces while mudlarking. The first two I pulled out of the soft mud, filled the palm of my hand. The shells were wavy and rough on the outside, and a gleaming pearly-white inside. Like the rings inside tree trunks, an oyster shell's layers tell the story of their life. They can indicate how fast they grew, whether the seasons were hot or cold, if they met any obstacles they had to grow around, or if their shell became attached to another oyster's shell.

Oyster colonies release sperm into the water, fertilizing the eggs that the female native oysters will keep inside their shell until they hatch

For a short time, tiny oysters have a foot that helps them swim and move across the sand and rocks until they find a place to settle

Oysters fix themselves permanently to a rock or another oyster, the foot disappears and a shell starts to grow

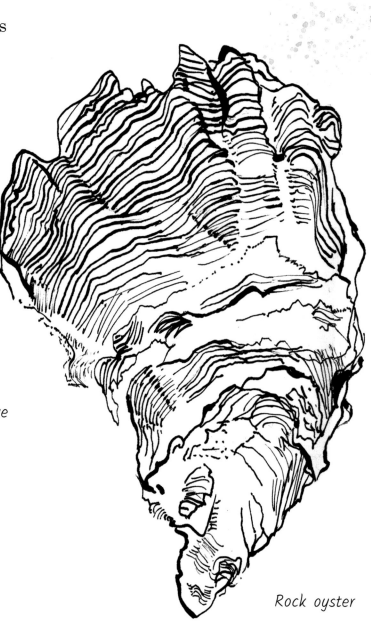

Rock oyster

The first shells I found were rock or Pacific oysters, which originated in Japanese waters. I soon discovered native oyster shells and began to learn about their history.

Oysters play a significant role in the ecosystem of the river and sea. They are filter feeders, pumping water in and out of their shells as they eat tiny plants and animals that are invisible to us. This process cleans the water as they filter out plankton, excess nutrients, and waste. Anything they don't eat sinks to the bottom, helping create a clean and healthy environment.

Native oysters are smoother and rounder than rock oysters (named for their rocky texture)

Gills

Tentacles

Digestive system

Heart

Hinge →

Oyster colonies also attach to each other, and any hard, submerged surface, to form reefs. These make excellent habitats for small fish, animals, larvae, or other crustaceans.

Oysters Now and Then

Native oysters have been living in and around the estuary for thousands of years, and they have always been a part of our diet.

Modern oyster dredging boat

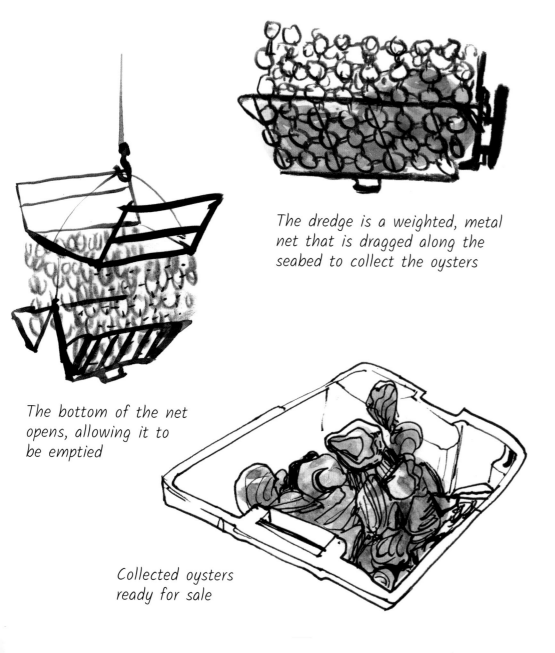

The dredge is a weighted, metal net that is dragged along the seabed to collect the oysters

The bottom of the net opens, allowing it to be emptied

Collected oysters ready for sale

Shells have been found in the remains of prehistoric villages; the Romans recorded how delicious they found Essex oysters; oysters were served to Shakespeare's audiences; and the poor bought them regularly on the streets of Victorian London—raw, cooked, in pies and stews—oysters were in abundance. At four for a penny, they ate millions of them!

Today, hardly anyone eats them, and oysters are considered a luxury. Why this change? Perhaps because the numbers of native oysters have dropped by almost 95 percent since the mid-1800s due to overfishing, pollution, and damage to their habitat. Now we are in danger of losing them altogether.

Oysters are a super-healthy food that can be harvested and farmed sustainably. This is happening now with the help of strict new laws and licenses. Reviving oyster populations will also bring benefits like increasing biodiversity.

While keeping their skills and traditions alive, oystermen close to the Thames Estuary are working with conservationists to protect the habitat of the native oyster.

Traditional oyster smack

Avocets

On the north and south banks of the Thames, avocets can be found in the salt marshes that soak up the tides. These tall, elegant wading birds vanished from the UK in the 1800s, mainly due to the destruction of their wetland habitat. Then, during the Second World War, the coastal marshes were flooded in hopes of making it difficult for the enemy to invade by boat. This turned out to be the invitation the avocets needed, and they returned to the Thames Estuary in large flocks. Since that time, people have successfully encouraged them to stay by protecting this habitat.

In winter, they gather in large flocks, then in spring they begin to nest in pairs. Avocets are ground-nesting birds, which means they lay their eggs in a dip in the earth or pebbly ground, and lined with a few sticks and grasses. They're often well hidden, but they are vulnerable to predators like foxes and crows. Their eggs are pale cream with dark brown speckles camouflaging them.

With their black and white plumage, avocets stand out from other wading birds. They totter on their stilt-like legs and tip forward to swish their curved bills back and forth in the water. Stirring it up, they make a meal out of any insects, worms, and crustaceans that they can catch.

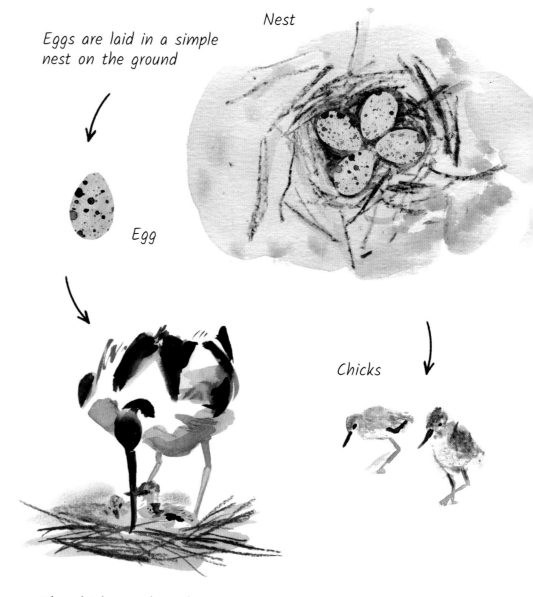

Eggs are laid in a simple nest on the ground

Nest

Egg

Chicks

The chicks are born less than a month later and immediately follow the mother out of the nest

Their distinctive bill
curves up at the end

Their bold black
and white feathers
help camouflage
the birds

Long powder-blue legs

Salt Marshes and Mudflats

Flocks of wading birds gather as the tide goes out on the Hoo Peninsula marshes between the Thames and Medway estuaries. Standing in rows along the silver lines of water as it slips away, they watch for little creatures left behind in the mud.

Many birds on the marshes are vulnerable to attack by birds of prey. You can tell when marsh harriers are near because the air is suddenly full of flapping wings. The contrasting black and white feathers of avocets and lapwings create an optical illusion that hides their individual silhouettes, making them more difficult to catch. Other birds find shelter in the reeds and scrub.

Curlew

Curlews are the largest wading birds in the UK, a threatened species struggling to survive due to predators and loss of habitat. At least they have a safe place to spend winters along the quieter parts of the Thames.

Listen for their rippling *curlee curlee curl curl curl* whistle day and night.

Dunlin

Greenshank

Godwit

Lapwing

Oystercatcher

Knot

Plover

Redshank

Lapwings in flight

On the ground, they are small and still. In flight, their open wings flap like huge, dark paddles rowing through the air.

You can also see lapwings here, facing into the wind that ruffles their long, fine crests. They sometimes look black and white, but when the sunlight catches their feathers, they shine a glorious purple and green.

Cormorant drying its wings

Here are two examples of diving birds that hunt for food underwater

Tufted ducks

Female

Male

The Sea

The Thames gradually widens and, along with other
rivers from the north and south, it joins the North Sea.
Our fascinating journey ends not at a single point or
instant, but dissolves hypnotically into the sea. For miles
and miles, water and land mix and mingle to create infinite
islands and underwater meadows that we can reach only
with our imagination.

Threats to the Thames

In this book we have taken a journey through different habitats and have seen just a few of the hundreds of species that the Thames supports. Though some are less polluted than they once were, many of these habitats and species are still under threat.

Sewage

The Thames sewage system in London was built for a population less than half its current size. As a result, millions of tons of raw, untreated sewage spill into the River Thames each year.

The Thames Tideway Tunnel being built in London will be 15.5 miles long and—once completed—should capture 95 percent of the sewage spills. It should significantly improve water quality and create a much healthier environment for wildlife.

Pesticides

Pesticides used in farming can drain into rivers from the surrounding land. These pollutants can change the chemical make-up of the water and harm wildlife. Insects provide the main source of food for many fish and birds, and can transmit high levels of chemicals. Restricting the use of pesticides is essential for keeping the river's ecosystem in balance.

Plastics

You will see litter along the riverbanks and in the water. Plastic takes hundreds of years to break down. Single-use plastics like food packaging and drink bottles are major threats to wildlife. Tiny plastic fibers are mistaken by fish for food. They can deplete nutrients, block stomachs and intestines, and cause choking. Microfibers that aren't trapped in sewage systems are released into the rivers when synthetic fabrics are machine washed. Acrylic clothing gives off the most plastic particles. Wet wipes are also a huge problem. If flushed down the toilet, they can end up in our rivers. Wet wipes have built up in places on the banks of the Thames, changing the course of the river, and impacting wildlife.

Invasive species

An increase in travel and transportation has allowed many non-native species of plants and animals to settle along our riverbanks and in rivers. They can reproduce rapidly as they have no natural predators, and threaten our native species. Invasive species on the Thames include buddleia, pennywort, Himalayan balsam, Japanese knotweed, quagga mussel, and signal crayfish.

Rivers act as dispersion corridors and enable invasive species to spread to areas where they can thrive. Careful introduction of plants or animals that feed on these invasive species can help. At present, many must be removed by hand.

Climate change

Climate change has a catastrophic effect on ecosystems like rivers. The Thames is getting warmer at an average of 0.36°F each year, damaging habitats and wildlife. Water levels are also rising in the Thames, which can lead to flooded lowlands, displaced wetlands, and changes to the tidal range.

Many native plants will not survive a rise in temperature as the land heats up. Animals that rely on the river for food, water, and shelter may find the river is no longer able to sustain their needs. As well as reducing carbon emissions to slow climate change, we need to restore carbon-capturing habitats through *rewilding* schemes.

A recent restoration project at the Greenwich Peninsula created saltmarsh terraces, which are effective at storing carbon, and reedbeds to encourage native species to colonize the area.

Conservation

Many people are working hard to make our rivers cleaner and restore natural habitats, enabling wildlife to thrive.

Restoring rivers

In the past, gravel was dredged from rivers for use in building and road construction. Restoring it provides habitats for fish to spawn. Reinstating the way a river naturally meanders helps with water flow, reduces bank erosion, and offers new habitats for wildlife.

Reedbeds

Reedbeds provide a natural filter for oxygenating water and removing pollutants. Native plants along our riverbanks protect wildlife and help bind the banks together to stop erosion. There are numerous projects on the Thames to plant new reedbeds and reinstate old ones.

Wetlands

Wetlands support a diverse number of species, storing and filtering water, and capturing carbon dioxide. Unfortunately, wetlands continue to be drained causing devastation to wildlife. A recent project near Oxford established a new water course that has bypassed a dam and reestablished a large floodplain. Fish can now swim this almost 19 mile stretch and spawn for the first time in more than a century.

Corridors

River corridors are necessary for animals to move safely between habitats. Young fish rely on the shallows of the Upper Thames and the reedbeds of the marshy estuary for protection. Some spend their lives in the sea and then swim upriver to breed, while others travel the opposite direction. Man-made barriers like dams and locks often block these journeys. River obstructions critically endanger eels. Conservation groups are working to set up safe passageways around dams and locks to enable the eels to travel freely.

Planting trees

The trees along our riverbanks slow the flow of water, which helps manage flood risk. They provide shade, which cools the water and helps improve water quality. This contributes to the wellbeing of wildlife and benefits us. Many tree species are being devastated by disease, so planting new trees and replacing old ones is crucial.

Citizen science

Citizen science is scientific research carried out by the general public. Conservation projects often involve surveys before a plan of action is drawn up. This allows scientists to gather information on a scale that they could never achieve alone. The people taking part observe, record, and submit data, which helps identify issues. There are lots of citizen science projects locally and online.

What you can do to help

There are many ways that you can help improve rivers, by yourself, as a family, or as a classroom project. Most tap water is supplied by reservoirs filled by rivers and streams. When these reservoirs run short of water due to a drought, it impacts the environment and the animals that rely on the river.

Save water at home by using a dish pan when washing dishes and reuse this wastewater for your plants. Wash your clothes less frequently. Turn off the tap while you brush your teeth and take shorter showers.

Find official organizations online or in your local community that need your support.

- Volunteer for a litter clean-up to help protect local wildlife and make friends in the process!
- Keep a wildlife diary, make notes, sketches or videos, recording observations when visiting wildlife areas.
- Participate in wildlife counts.
- Report sightings of varied species to increase awareness for local projects.
- Volunteer to help remove invasive plant species.
- Protect the environment from plastic pollution by always taking your litter home with you.
- Pressure policy makers and manufacturers to address conservation issues and to act responsibly.
- Raise money and awareness for environmental charities.
- Get involved!

Notebook

Here are some of my favorite drawings from my notebooks, done in watercolor, pencil, pen, and ink

Finding the right materials to show the bright, jewel colors of dragonflies and damselflies

The summer view from a favorite camping spot on the Thames near Goring

Forget-me-nots

Bearded tits on the marshes, balancing on swaying reeds, eating seeds to survive through winter

A curlew spotted on the east coast of England

These distinctive wading birds are in decline, so I felt privileged to live where their calls could be heard throughout the night, the sounds skipping across the moonlit marshes

A black-headed gull with summer plumage,
in winter their heads are white

Swans flying in V formation.
Listen for the beating of their
huge wings!

Research for this book included
hundreds of hours of drawing, reading,
and exploring the River Thames

Admiring the colorful boats

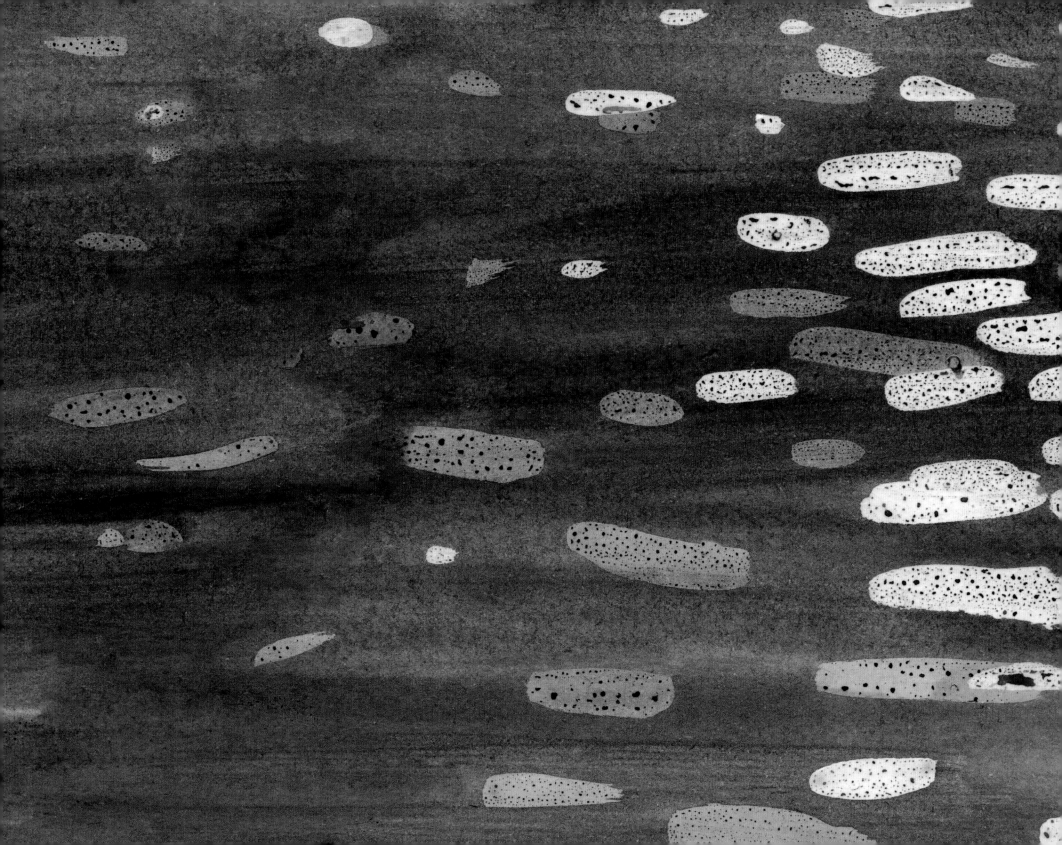